Mostly
CONVERSATION
Materials for the ESL Classroom

By Doraina Pyle

Contents

Back in Black

Templates

Board Games – 3 Options

Group Project Ideas

Skit/Play

Illustrated Short Story

New Product/Feature

Plan a Party

Create an Ideal City

Create an English Language Learning Game

GOALS

I want to:

To reach my goal(s), I need to:

1.

2.

3.

My target date to reach my goal(s):

THE DICE GAME

Other materials: Dice

Activity: Break students into partners or groups. Have them rotate rolling a die to ask and answer the questions below using the *simple present*.

What do you do...	What do you do...
1- In the morning? 2- Everyday? 3- Each Tuesday? 4- On the weekend? 5- At night? 6- Every year?	1- In the morning? 2- Everyday? 3- Each Tuesday? 4- On the weekend? 5- At night? 6- Every year?
What do you do... 1- In the morning? 2- Everyday? 3- Each Tuesday? 4- On the weekend? 5- At night? 6- Every year?	What do you do... 1- In the morning? 2- Everyday? 3- Each Tuesday? 4- On the weekend? 5- At night? 6- Every year?
What do you do... 1- In the morning? 2- Everyday? 3- Each Tuesday? 4- On the weekend? 5- At night? 6- Every year?	What do you do... 1- In the morning? 2- Everyday? 3- Each Tuesday? 4- On the weekend? 5- At night? 6- Every year?

THE CARD GAME

Other materials: None

Activity: Place all cards into a pile. Have students draw and answer questions using the *simple present*.

IN THE MORNING?	IN THE AFTERNOON?	IN THE EVENING?
EVERYDAY?	EVERY MONDAY?	EVERY TUESDAY?
EACH WEDNESDAY?	EACH THURSDAY?	EACH FRIDAY?

WHAT DO
YOU DO...

WHAT DO
YOU DO...

WHAT DO
YOU DO...

WHAT DO
YOU DO...

WHAT DO
YOU DO...

WHAT DO
YOU DO...

WHAT DO
YOU DO...

WHAT DO
YOU DO...

WHAT DO
YOU DO...

ON SATURDAY?	ON SUNDAY?	ON THE WEEKEND?
AT NIGHT?	EVERY WEEK?	EVERY MONTH?
EVERY YEAR?	AT WORK?	AT HOME?

WHAT DO YOU DO...

WHAT DO YOU DO...

WHAT DO YOU DO...

WHAT DO YOU DO...

WHAT DO YOU DO...

WHAT DO YOU DO...

WHAT DO YOU DO...

WHAT DO YOU DO...

WHAT DO YOU DO...

AT SCHOOL?	FOR FUN?	IN SUMMER?
IN WINTER?	IN FALL?	IN SPRING?
EVERY 5 YEARS?	WHEN THE WEATHER IS NICE?	WHEN THE WEATHER IS BAD?

WHAT DO
YOU DO...

WHAT DO
YOU DO...

WHAT DO
YOU DO...

WHAT DO
YOU DO...

WHAT DO
YOU DO...

WHAT DO
YOU DO...

WHAT DO
YOU DO...

WHAT DO
YOU DO...

WHAT DO
YOU DO...

(Your idea)

WHAT DO
YOU DO...

WHAT DO
YOU DO...

WHAT DO
YOU DO...

WHAT DO
YOU DO...

WHAT DO
YOU DO...

WHAT DO
YOU DO...

WHAT DO
YOU DO...

WHAT DO
YOU DO...

WHAT DO
YOU DO...

The CARD Game — Take Two

Other materials: None

Activity: Have students draw action and question cards from a pile, using the first to answer the second with the **simple present**.

WHAT DOES HE DO?	WHAT DOES SHE DO?	WHAT DO THEY DO?
WHAT DOES HE DO?	WHAT DOES SHE DO?	WHAT DO THEY DO?
WHAT DOES HE DO?	WHAT DOES SHE DO?	WHAT DO THEY DO?

QUESTION   QUESTION   QUESTION

QUESTION   QUESTION   QUESTION

QUESTION   QUESTION   QUESTION

WHAT DO WE DO?	WHAT DO YOU DO?	WHAT DO I DO?
WHAT DO WE DO?	WHAT DO YOU DO?	WHAT DO I DO?
WHAT DO WE DO?	WHAT DO YOU DO?	WHAT DO I DO?

QUESTION   QUESTION   QUESTION

QUESTION   QUESTION   QUESTION

QUESTION   QUESTION   QUESTION

WALK A MILE	EAT SOME PIE	READ A BOOK
DANCE ALL NIGHT	WATCH A GOOD MOVIE	EXERCISE IN THE MORNING
SEND A TEXT	LISTEN TO THE RADIO	WRAP A PRESENT

ACTION   ACTION   ACTION

ACTION   ACTION   ACTION

ACTION   ACTION   ACTION

PLAY THE DRUMS	SING IN A BAND	OPEN A PRESENT
SLEEP ALL DAY	LOOK FOR A RAINBOW	MAKE DINNER
SWEEP THE PORCH	BUY A NEW CAR	DO THE LAUNDRY

ACTION ACTION ACTION

ACTION ACTION ACTION

ACTION ACTION ACTION

JUST MY IMAGINATION

Other materials: Pictures (IE from magazines)

Activity: Give each student a picture and a card. Have them create a "**backstory**" from what they see to present to the class.

Imagination Game

With the pictures that have been provided, use your imagination to tell me about the people therein.
(In other words, give me their story by making up answers.)

"What's his/her name?"

"Where is he/she from?"

"What does he/she do for work?"

"What does he/she like to do for fun?"

"Is he/she married?"

"How old is he/she?"

"Does he/she have any pets?"

"Does he/she play any sports? Which ones?"

"What kind of music does he/she like?"

Imagination Game

With the pictures that have been provided, use your imagination to tell me about the people therein.
(In other words, give me their story by making up answers.)

"What's his/her name?"

"Where is he/she from?"

"What does he/she do for work?"

"What does he/she like to do for fun?"

"Is he/she married?"

"How old is he/she?"

"Does he/she have any pets?"

"Does he/she play any sports? Which ones?"

"What kind of music does he/she like?"

CHARADES

Other materials: Bag

Activity: Place all actions into a bag. Have a student draw a task and act out what is listed. Ask "What is he/she doing?" and encourage other students to guess using complete sentences with the **present continuous (or progressive)**.

Brushing my teeth	Cleaning my room	Cooking a meal
Dancing	Doing homework	Drinking water
Driving a car	Eating	Feeding my dog
Fixing the sink	Jumping rope	Painting the wall
Playing soccer	Raising my hand	Reading a book
Singing a song	Swimming	Talking on the phone
Taking a nap	Washing the Dishes	Watching TV

Epic or Fail

Other materials: Red and green paper, popsicle sticks, glue, online video

Activity: Give each student a positive and negative sign (copied onto red and green paper respectively, then glued to popsicle sticks). Pull up an online video of the game "Epic or Fail." Have students 'predict' the *future* using their signs.

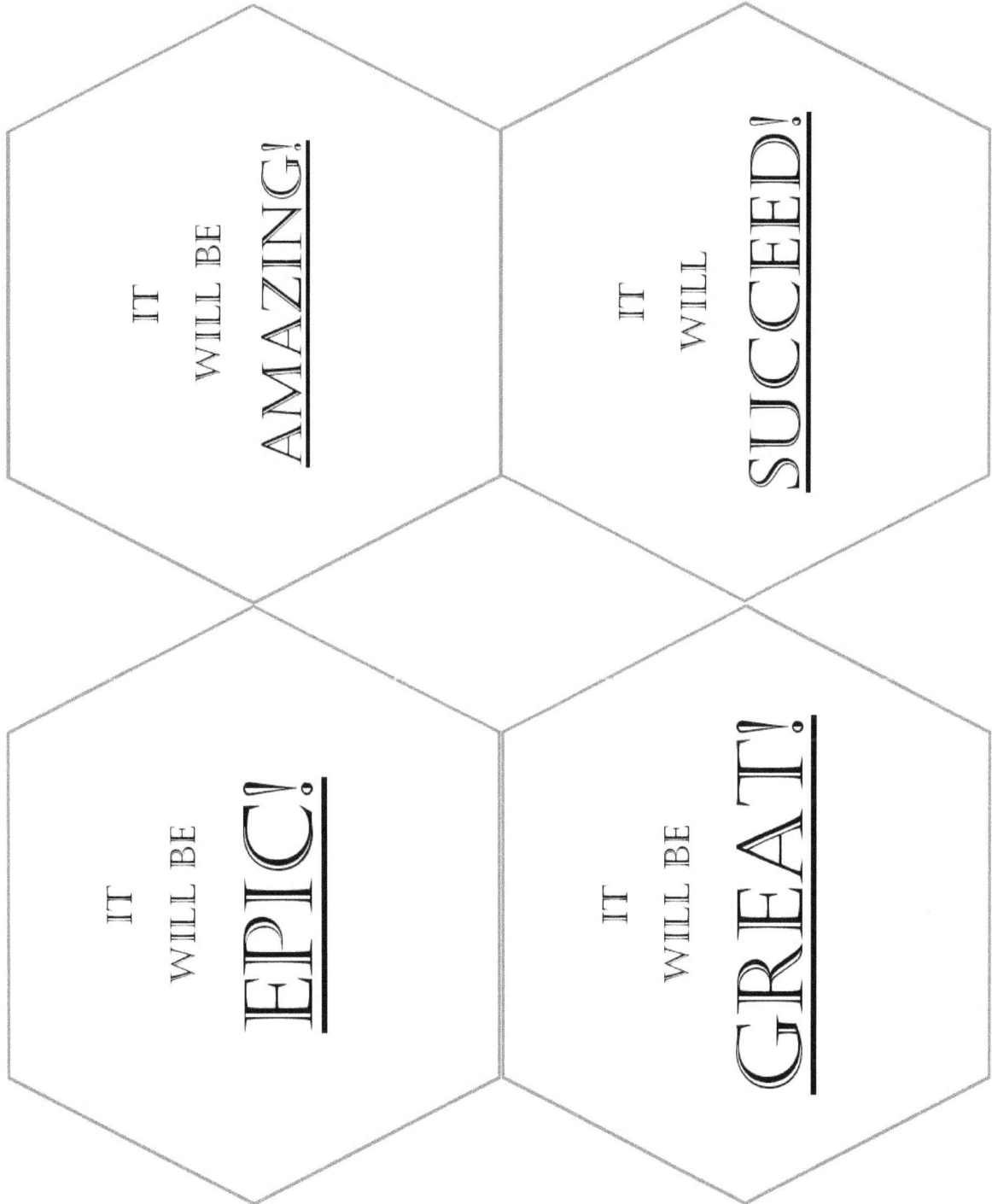

IT WILL BE **AMAZING!**

IT WILL **SUCCEED!**

IT WILL BE **EPIC!**

IT WILL BE **GREAT!**

IT
WILL BE A
DISASTER!

IT
WILL BE
REALLY
BAD!

IT
WILL BE
TERRIBLE!

IT
WILL
FAIL!

I SEE *THE FUTURE*!

Other materials: Spinner (or brad and paperclip for spinner)

Activity: Break students into partners. Have one student draw a "What will happen with...?" card from a pile and the other use the spinner and chart to provide a "You will" prediction.

Money?	**Love?**	**Work?**
My House?	**My Car?**	**The Weather?**
Children?	**Skills?**	**Family?**
Pets?	**Health?**	**Travel?**

What will happen
with…

What will happen
with…

What will happen
with…

What will happen
with…

What will happen
with…

What will happen
with…

What will happen
with…

What will happen
with…

What will happen
with…

What will happen
with…

What will happen
with…

What will happen
with…

Tell Me the Future

You will...

Money	**Love**	**Work**
A. Your idea	A. Marry for life	A. Manage a company
B. Win the Lottery	B. Your idea	B. Work many 12-hours
C. Have enough to pay your bills	C. Stay single	days
D. Lose all your savings at the casino	D. Experience some heartbreak	C. Your idea
E. Donate everything to the poor	E. Divorce 6 times	D. Be self-employed
		E. Become a beach bum

House	**Car**	**Weather**
A. Own a three-bedroom home	A. Ride a bike your entire life	A. Your idea
B. Live in a mansion in Malibu	B. Take the subway	B. See a hurricane
C. Set up a tent in your mother's backyard	C. Drive a BMW	C. Carry an umbrella with you everywhere
D. Your idea	D. Own a mini-van	D. Enjoy 70-degree weather
E. Rent a condo in Manhattan	E. Your idea	E. Build an igloo in some part of Siberia

Children	**Skills**	**Family**
A. Have 1 child	A. Learn to play guitar	A. Attend reunions 3 times a year
B. Your idea	B. Sing a solo in class	B. See your family at Christmas
C. Adopt 16 children	C. Your idea	C. Move far, far away
D. Have 9 children	D. Become an ambassador to the US because of your mad English skills	D. Your idea
E. Have no children	E. Keep everything a secret	E. Have everyone live at your house

Pets	**Health**	**Travel**
A. Have no pets	A. Your idea	A. Venture around the world
B. Adopt 7 dogs and 6 cats	B. Battle measles, mumps & bird flu	B. Your idea
C. Own 2 goldfish	C. Find the cure to cancer	C. Go no where
D. Carry a parrot on your shoulder	D. Be immune to all disease	D. Visit a few countries
E. Your idea	E. Live to be 108 years old	E. Tour the same small town over-and-over again

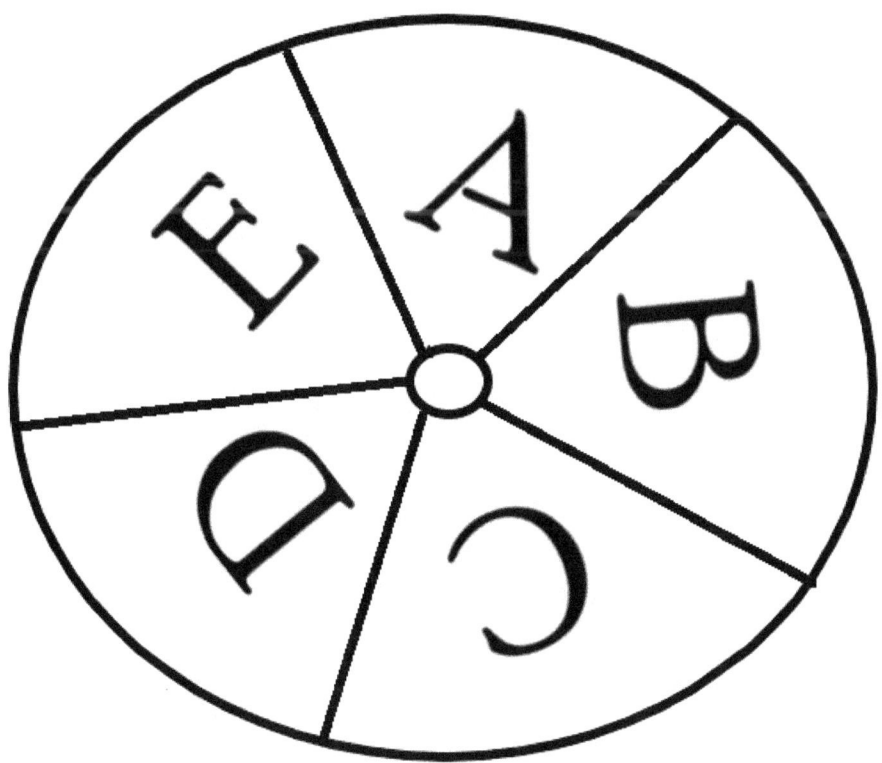

Bingo

Other materials: Bag, paper pieces (to cover or daub the words), whiteboard, marker, prizes

Activity: Put cut-up verb list into a bag. Give each student a Bingo card and some paper pieces. Draw and call out base verbs one at a time. Have students cover the **past tense** forms of the verb on their cards. When a student gets five in a row (horizontally, vertically, or diagonally), he shouts "Bingo!" and wins a prize.

Extra: Write both forms of the verb on a whiteboard, if possible (IE ask → asked). When finished with the game, have students make sentences with the verbs and put them on the board.

BINGO VERB LIST

ASK	CREATE	HELP	SEE
BECOME	DRAW	KNOW	SEND
BEGIN	DRIVE	MAKE	SPEAK
BELIEVE	FEEL	MEET	STUDY
BREAK	FIND	NEED	TAKE
BRING	GET	PAY	THINK
BUILD	GIVE	PLAY	TRY
BUY	GO	PUT	WANT
CALL	GROW	READ	WATCH
COME	HAPPEN	RUN	WORK
COOK	HEAR	SAY	WRITE

PAST TENSE BINGO

asked	became	believed	worked	saw
met	happened	wanted	helped	spoke
created	wrote	Free	said	grew
made	paid	sent	called	broke
cooked	felt	brought	tried	came

PAST TENSE BINGO

played	said	made	went	took
came	brought	knew	cooked	needed
got	saw	Free	found	thought
began	wrote	put	met	gave
spoke	read	watched	drove	helped

PAST TENSE BINGO

read	began	believed	gave	cooked
put	drove	heard	bought	got
built	played	Free	said	met
wrote	tried	took	wanted	studied
asked	thought	sent	ran	made

PAST TENSE BINGO

needed	studied	built	sent	ran
believed	called	watched	read	asked
became	drew	Free	happened	paid
saw	took	went	created	began
spoke	got	broke	came	helped

Past Tense Bingo

read	came	worked	went	built
bought	heard	called	watched	thought
ran	spoke	Free	paid	studied
felt	saw	said	broke	asked
met	knew	put	believed	played

Past Tense Bingo

gave	cooked	helped	worked	put
grew	made	said	needed	thought
broke	brought	Free	felt	drew
tried	became	heard	met	found
took	wanted	paid	drove	began

Past Tense Bingo

took	cooked	met	felt	found
tried	got	needed	worked	began
saw	thought	Free	drew	paid
created	asked	gave	built	brought
bought	became	broke	played	studied

Past Tense Bingo

knew	helped	asked	felt	studied
drove	sent	ran	read	began
bought	watched	Free	created	wrote
wanted	spoke	built	made	paid
grew	put	believed	went	broke

PAST TENSE BINGO

heard	said	built	wrote	read
asked	spoke	came	became	created
made	helped	Free	saw	began
drew	cooked	happened	bought	broke
knew	took	grew	felt	went

PAST TENSE BINGO

met	went	put	happened	wanted
tried	found	studied	called	played
watched	grew	Free	read	created
ran	made	came	asked	built
worked	needed	cooked	heard	paid

Past Tense Bingo

asked	heard	made	put	drove
saw	paid	felt	built	became
called	got	Free	went	sent
happened	came	met	believed	tried
said	began	spoke	read	drew

Past Tense Bingo

studied	thought	broke	needed	believed
took	helped	brought	knew	got
gave	paid	Free	watched	found
built	played	met	tried	worked
went	wrote	sent	made	put

PAST TENSE BINGO

worked	got	tried	cooked	wanted
played	drove	took	brought	heard
said	wrote	Free	ran	saw
asked	became	studied	created	put
helped	read	watched	came	found

PAST TENSE BINGO

gave	wanted	became	made	created
spoke	believed	called	grew	felt
broke	found	Free	read	asked
cooked	knew	watched	helped	met
came	wrote	thought	happened	heard

PAST TENSE BINGO

met	built	studied	found	grew
watched	needed	broke	created	believed
took	drew	Free	brought	felt
got	helped	paid	called	thought
heard	gave	cooked	played	asked

PAST TENSE BINGO

brought	became	broke	drew	took
knew	tried	put	grew	made
thought	sent	Free	spoke	began
drove	played	met	came	believed
studied	bought	saw	wanted	needed

PAST TENSE BINGO

wrote	asked	created	needed	brought
began	helped	said	saw	became
drove	made	Free	sent	spoke
believed	felt	broke	happened	took
met	found	paid	studied	got

PAST TENSE BINGO

found	asked	got	worked	read
went	felt	put	wrote	wanted
called	watched	Free	came	happened
built	ran	bought	cooked	saw
drew	heard	tried	grew	became

PAST TENSE BINGO

put	broke	called	believed	brought
grew	went	read	made	watched
came	wanted	Free	happened	got
ran	tried	knew	worked	spoke
drove	cooked	heard	built	began

PAST TENSE BINGO

put	brought	studied	thought	paid
broke	built	played	asked	ran
became	tried	Free	said	called
read	bought	needed	cooked	found
helped	began	went	drew	gave

PAST TENSE BINGO

wrote	bought	gave	drew	thought
knew	sent	began	worked	drove
made	spoke	**Free**	believed	felt
helped	met	studied	broke	went
found	brought	needed	put	became

PAST TENSE BINGO

spoke	said	happened	came	wrote
asked	made	helped	saw	believed
watched	sent	**Free**	met	heard
created	got	became	felt	studied
gave	built	broke	worked	played

PAST TENSE BINGO

made	heard	ran	cooked	sent
said	asked	worked	became	felt
got	created	**Free**	played	wrote
happened	took	believed	grew	paid
met	needed	helped	came	bought

PAST TENSE BINGO

wanted	got	believed	asked	took
paid	said	began	gave	thought
went	tried	**Free**	played	called
read	grew	knew	sent	drove
built	put	came	brought	watched

PAST TENSE BINGO

made	became	got	brought	took
ran	paid	studied	thought	wrote
gave	created	Free	began	watched
spoke	built	drew	found	called
asked	played	read	wanted	went

PAST TENSE BINGO

tried	believed	drew	knew	came
began	grew	drove	saw	made
took	broke	Free	worked	found
met	got	played	needed	sent
wanted	wrote	heard	studied	thought

PAST TENSE BINGO

knew	asked	helped	wrote	drove
created	drew	got	built	tried
sent	believed	Free	went	heard
began	made	cooked	spoke	saw
felt	worked	met	broke	said

PAST TENSE BINGO

cooked	tried	went	sent	paid
put	wanted	made	called	grew
studied	became	Free	bought	met
read	watched	ran	came	began
happened	found	gave	worked	took

PAST TENSE BINGO

thought	said	tried	bought	came
felt	went	worked	sent	made
put	drew	Free	wanted	paid
called	brought	read	studied	asked
began	watched	played	grew	happened

PAST TENSE BINGO

saw	studied	wanted	brought	believed
put	heard	wrote	needed	helped
went	took	Free	paid	drove
built	spoke	created	became	thought
got	broke	gave	found	called

PAST TENSE BINGO

wrote	read	knew	needed	became
drove	spoke	began	bought	sent
saw	found	Free	made	gave
brought	thought	paid	got	called
took	played	broke	built	grew

PAST TENSE BINGO

wanted	sent	came	drew	felt
became	cooked	watched	thought	worked
wrote	studied	Free	paid	heard
put	helped	built	knew	said
got	brought	ran	tried	happened

PAST TENSE BINGO

began	said	knew	believed	created
sent	became	saw	tried	wrote
spoke	made	Free	heard	drove
drew	helped	studied	met	felt
needed	happened	found	broke	ran

PAST TENSE BINGO

went	brought	bought	tried	helped
called	wanted	asked	paid	ran
met	read	Free	grew	put
needed	wrote	began	believed	watched
cooked	sent	worked	happened	came

PAST TENSE BINGO

called	watched	bought	tried	broke
heard	created	brought	wanted	began
met	happened	Free	sent	drove
played	took	said	knew	ran
believed	cooked	paid	gave	needed

PAST TENSE BINGO

broke	called	played	gave	drove
tried	knew	bought	worked	felt
heard	thought	Free	found	helped
spoke	grew	created	went	got
drew	happened	studied	became	read

(Your idea)

PAST TENSE BINGO

		Free		

PAST TENSE BINGO

		Free		

WHEEL OF PAST TIMES

Other materials: Spinner (or brad and paper clip for spinner)

Activity: Divide students into partners or groups. Have one student spin and ask the question and another student answer using the *past tense*.

Note: Larger version on next page.

Where did you go...?

What did you do...?

What did you do...?

in winter?

in (year)?

as a child?

in (month)?

yesterday?

Where did you go...?

last night?

when it last rained?

last week?

What did you do...

this morning?

on (day of the week)?

earlier today?

a month ago?

in summer?

last year?

when it last rained?

at (time)?

What did you do...?

Where did you go...?

What did you do...?

Where did you go...?

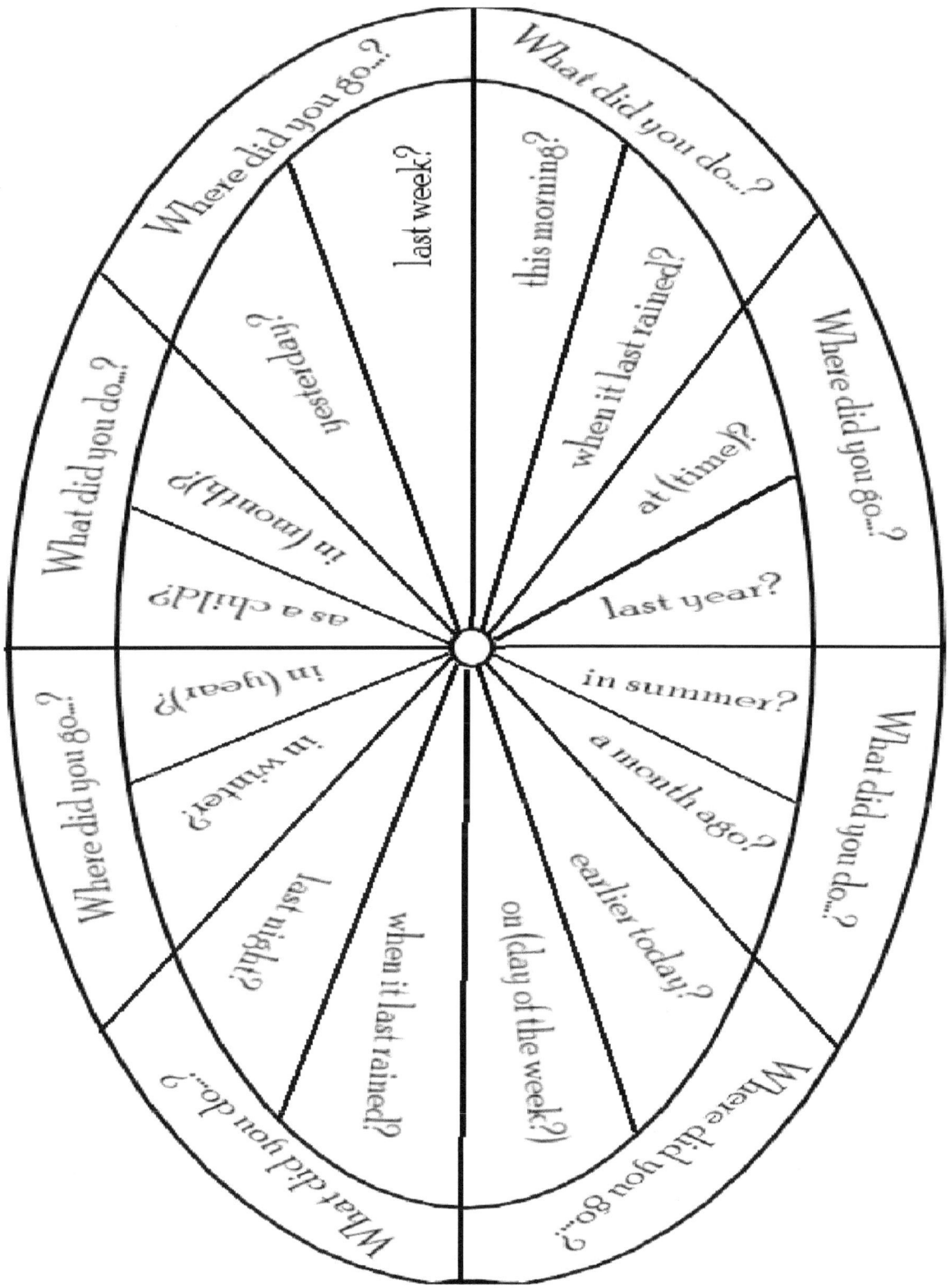

Where did you go...?

What did you do...?

last week?

this morning?

when it last rained?

at (time)?

Where did you go...?

What did you do...?

yesterday?

in (month)?

as a child?

last year?

in (year)?

in summer?

Where did you go...?

in winter?

a month ago?

What did you do...?

last night?

when it last rained?

earlier today?

on (day of the week)?

What did you do...?

Where did you go...?

TIC TAC TOE

Other materials: None

Activity: Break students into partners. Give them the X and O pieces (next pages). To play, a student must make a sentence using the past participle (from any **perfect tense**) on his game piece. The first student to get three in a row (horizontally, vertically, or diagonally) wins the game.

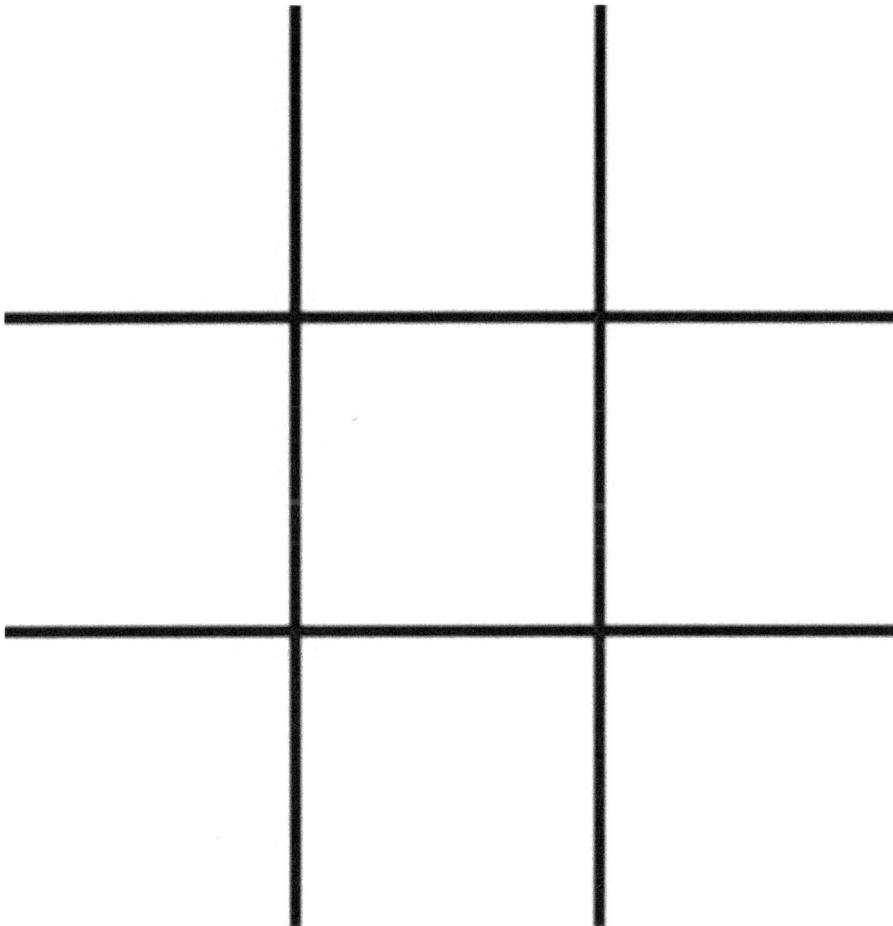

TIC TAC TOE

Game Pieces

Been	Bought	Cost
Become	Played	Done
Begun	Wanted	Said
Broken	Written	Seen
Brought	Come	Made
Built	Visited	Spoken

Cut	Forgotten	Cooked
Driven	Given	Known
Eaten	Gone	Stolen
Fallen	Had	Paid
Felt	Worked	Sung
Found	Talked	Taken

How long...?

Other materials: None

Activity: Break students into groups. Have them draw and answer questions using the *Present Perfect*.

... have you had your phone?	...have you lived in your house (or apartment)?	...have you known your best friend?
...have you played sports?	...have you studied English?	...have you been awake?
...have you cooked?	... have you sat today?	...have you felt the way you do about _____?

 HOW LONG...

 HOW LONG...

 HOW LONG...

 HOW LONG...

 HOW LONG...

 HOW LONG...

 HOW LONG...

 HOW LONG...

 HOW LONG...

... have you been alive?	...have you had this haircut?	... have you been married?
...have you been interested in your profession?	...have you lived in this city?	...have you driven?
...have you had your job?	...have you kept a gift?	...have you had your car?

How long...   How long...   How long...

How long...   How long...   How long...

How long...   How long...   How long...

… have you been able to swim?	…have you run errands today?	…have you slept?
…have you made _____?	…have you gone without _____?	…have you thought about _____?
…have you (Your idea)?	… have you (Your idea)?	…have you (Your idea)?

 HOW LONG...

 HOW LONG...

 HOW LONG...

 HOW LONG...

 HOW LONG...

 HOW LONG...

 HOW LONG...

 HOW LONG...

 HOW LONG...

ROCK AROUND THE CLOCK

Other materials: Spinner (or brad and paperclip for spinner)

Activity: Break students into partners or groups. Have them take turns spinning the wheel and asking and answering with the *past continuous*.

What were you doing at...

The Past ○ Continuous...

12

3

6

9

yesterday, last year, this morning...?

...SDM I

SDM I

SDM I

SDM I

I was...

I was...

I was...

I was...

I was...

I was...

I was...

MATCH-UP

Other materials: None

Activity: Set pieces onto a flat surface. Have students match each word with the correct *part of speech*.

The boy	*Noun*	A house	*Noun*
He	*Pronoun*	You	*Pronoun*
Eats	*Verb*	Run	*Verb*
Large	*Adjective*	Beautiful	*Adjective*
Quickly	*Adverb*	Fast	*Adverb*
At	*Preposition*	In	*Preposition*
And	*Conjunction*	Or	*Conjunction*
Ha-ha	*Interjection*	Eek	*Interjection*

(Your ideas)

	Noun		Noun
	Pronoun		Pronoun
	Verb		Verb
	Adjective		Adjective
	Adverb		Adverb
	Preposition		Preposition
	Conjunction		Conjunction
	Interjection		Interjection

PICTURE-ADJ

Other materials: Possible hat

Activity: Place all ***descriptions*** into a hat. Break students into teams and have them stand in lines at the board, ready to relay race. Call out a description. The person who draws it the fastest wins the point.

A TALL MAN HOLDING A CANE
A WOMAN WITH ONE EYE
A SKINNY TEENAGER ON A CELLPHONE
A LITTLE BOY CARRYING AN OVERSIZED TEDDY BEAR
A YOUNG GIRL IN PIGTAILS
A TODDLER WITH A MUSTACHE
A BABY WITH A WOODEN LEG
TWO GIRLS WITH BEARDS
SIX BOYS CARRYING WATERMELONS
THREE LARGE MEN WITH FLOWERS
FOUR WOMEN IN HIGH HEELS
A VERY LONG DOG WEARING A BOW TIE
A CAT ON CRUTCHES
A HORSE WITH TWO NOSES
A PIG IN PANTS AND A BLOUSE
A KID CARRYING AN UMBRELLA
A COW IN CURLERS
A GRANDMA WITH A HAIRNET
A RAT WEARING A MINI-SKIRT

GUESS WHO?

Other materials: Possible hat

Activity: Give each student a card. Have everyone pick another person in the room **_to describe_**. Tell students to mark the card as appropriate by filling in the blanks, circling, or putting a checkmark. Either collect the cards (and draw them out of a hat), or have students present their person themselves while everyone else guesses.

Pick a person in the room to describe. Mark below as appropriate.

This person is wearing…

- ☐ _____ jeans
  (color)
- ☐ a _____ shirt
- ☐ a _____ dress / skirt
- ☐ a _____ jacket
- ☐ a _____ necklace
- ☐ a _____ ring
- ☐ _____ earrings
- ☐ tennis shoes, sandals, high heels (circle)

This person has…

- ☐ _____ eyes
  (color)
- ☐ glasses
- ☐ braces
- ☐ a ponytail, bun, or braids (circle)
- ☐ dimples
- ☐ a mustache
- ☐ a beard
- ☐ tattoos… How many? ____ Where? _____
- ☐ Straight or curly hair? (circle)
- ☐ Long or short hair? (circle)

This person is (circle)

- ☐ Tall or short?
- ☐ Skinny or stocky?
- ☐ Young, middle-aged, or somewhat older?

Pick a person in the room to describe. Mark below as appropriate.

This person is wearing…

- ☐ _____ jeans
  (color)
- ☐ a _____ shirt
- ☐ a _____ dress / skirt
- ☐ a _____ jacket
- ☐ a _____ necklace
- ☐ a _____ ring
- ☐ _____ earrings
- ☐ tennis shoes, sandals, high heels (circle)

This person has…

- ☐ _____ eyes
  (color)
- ☐ glasses
- ☐ braces
- ☐ a ponytail, bun, or braids (circle)
- ☐ dimples
- ☐ a mustache
- ☐ a beard
- ☐ tattoos… How many? ____ Where? _____
- ☐ Straight or curly hair? (circle)
- ☐ Long or short hair? (circle)

This person is (circle)

- ☐ Tall or short?
- ☐ Skinny or stocky?
- ☐ Young, middle-aged, or somewhat older?

Twos and threes

Other materials: Items in Three (IE socks, candles, picture frames, bottles, dolls, hats, etc).

Activity: Have students work together to label and create sentences *by comparing objects* around and brought into the classroom.

Big	Bigger	Biggest
Black	Blacker	Blackest
Cheap	Cheaper	Cheapest
Clear	Clearer	Clearest
Cold	Colder	Coldest
Dirty	Dirtier	Dirtiest
Easy	Easier	Easiest
Great	Greater	Greatest
Happy	Happier	Happiest
Hard	Harder	Hardest
Heavy	Heavier	Heaviest
Hot	Hotter	Hottest
Light	Lighter	Lightest
Long	Longer	Longest
Loud	Louder	Loudest

Narrow	Narrower	Narrowest
New	Newer	Newest
Nice	Nicer	Nicest
Old	Older	Oldest
Quick	Quicker	Quickest
Quiet	Quieter	Quietest
Short	Shorter	Shortest
Slow	Slower	Slowest
Small	Smaller	Smallest
Soft	Softer	Softest
Tiny	Tinier	Tiniest
Ugly	Uglier	Ugliest
Good	Better	Best
Beautiful	More beautiful	Most beautiful
Expensive	More expensive	Most expensive
Important	More important	Most important
Wonderful	More wonderful	Most wonderful

Other materials: Classroom examples

Activity: Work together with students to label examples of **prepositions** found in the classroom.

ABOVE	AROUND
AT	BEHIND
BELOW	BESIDE
BETWEEN	FAR FROM
IN	INSIDE
NEAR	NEXT TO
ON	ON TOP OF
OUTSIDE	UNDER
IN FRONT OF	IN BACK OF

WHERE, OH WHERE?

Other materials: Pictures of places and streets, bags, possible blindfold

Activity: Either label or hang up cut-outs of typical businesses in town. Give each student the below questions (cut up in bags) and a list of *direction words*. Have one student draw a question and the other give directions as they walk to the location.

Extra: Have one student use a blindfold.

How do I get to the HOTEL?	How do I get to the FIRE STATION?	How do I get to the CINEMA?
Where can I find a RESTAURANT?	Where can I find a CHURCH?	Where is MAIN STREET?
Where can I find a BANK?	What's the best way to the POLICE STATION?	Where is the LIBRARY?
Can you tell me how to get to the COLLEGE?	What's the best way to the POST OFFICE?	Where is the CITY PARK?
Can you tell me how to get to the BAKERY?	What's the best way to the HOSPITAL?	Where am I?
Can you help me? I'm looking for the HIGH SCHOOL?	Can you help me? I'm looking for the SHOPPING MALL?	Where am I?

Where can I buy bread?	Where can I buy a stamp?	Where do I get clothes?
Where do the children play?	Where can I get medical treatment?	Where can I eat out?
Where can I buy groceries?	Where can I find entertainment?	Where's the best place to get donuts?

Places and streets

Hotel	Fire Station
Restaurant	Church
Bank	Police Station
College	Post Office
Bakery	Hospital
High School	Shopping Mall
Cinema	Library
City Park	Main Street
Peach Lane	Royal Road

Possible cut-outs

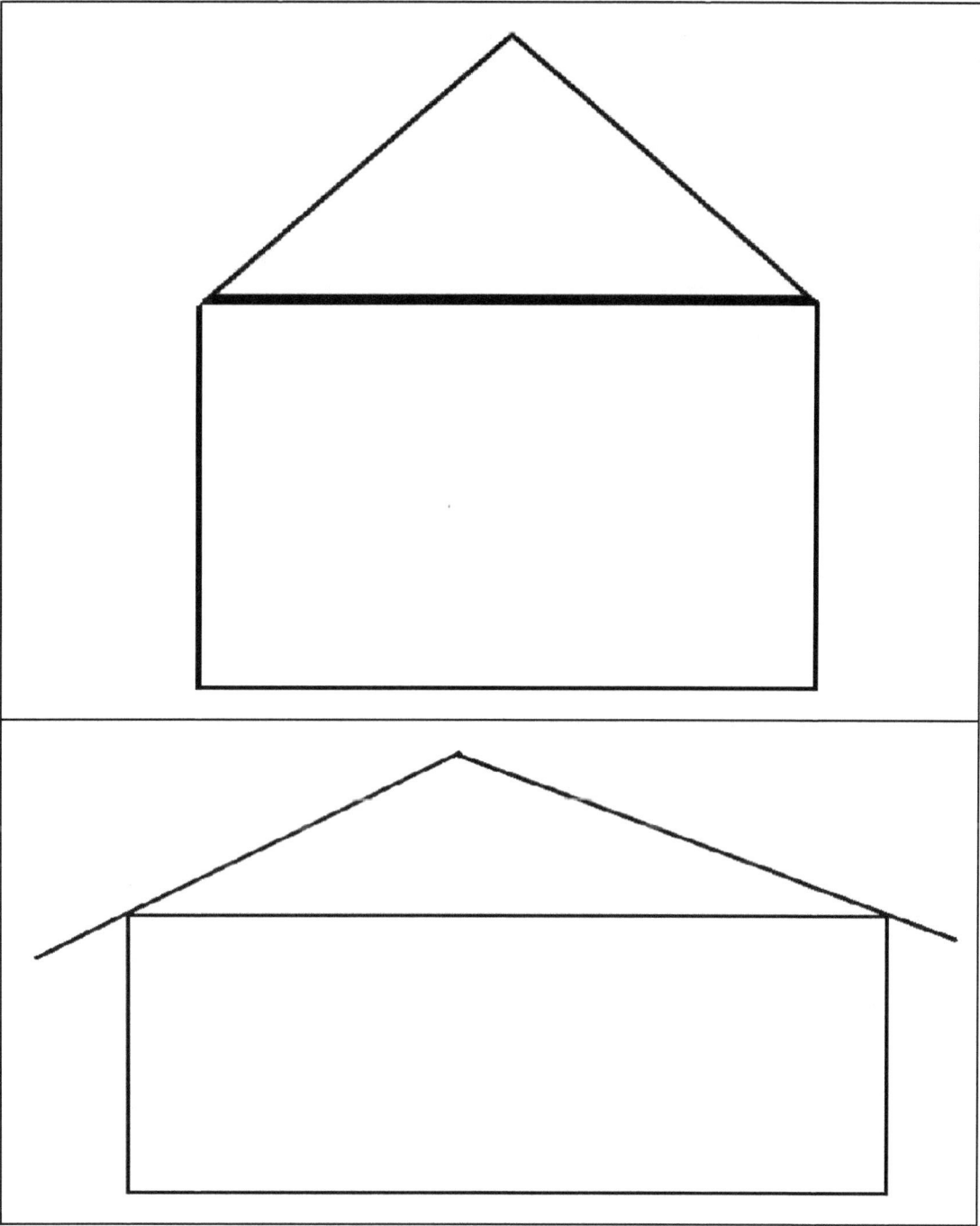

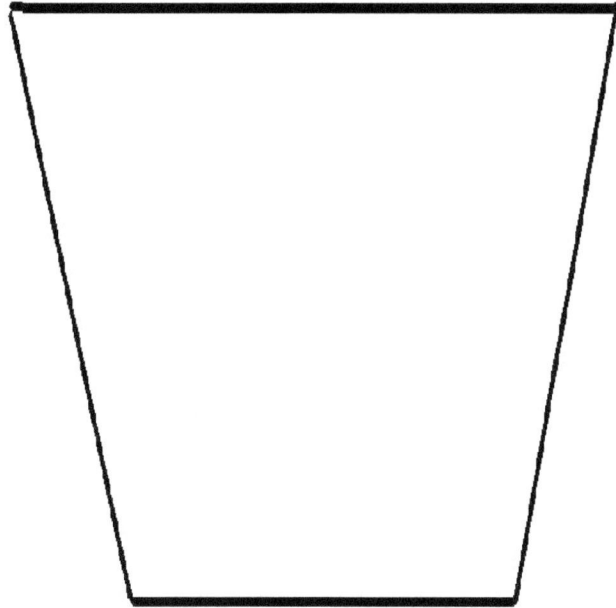

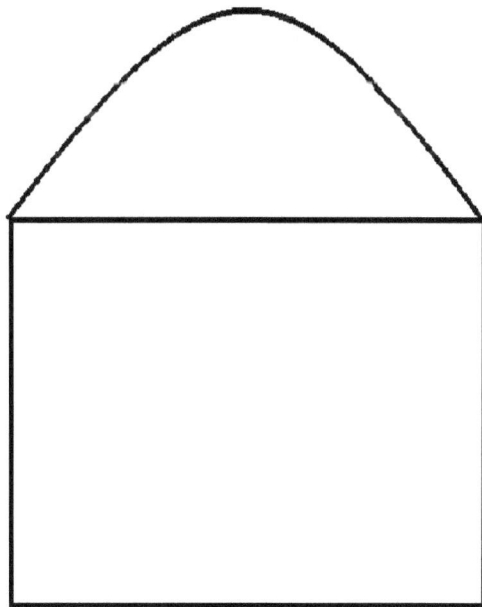

Direction Words

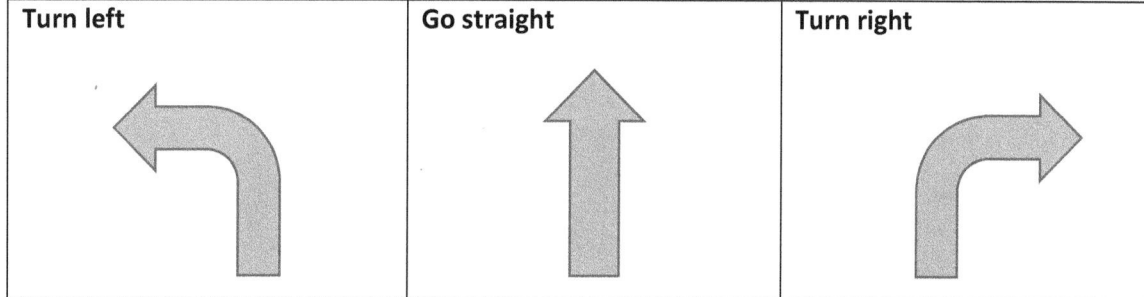

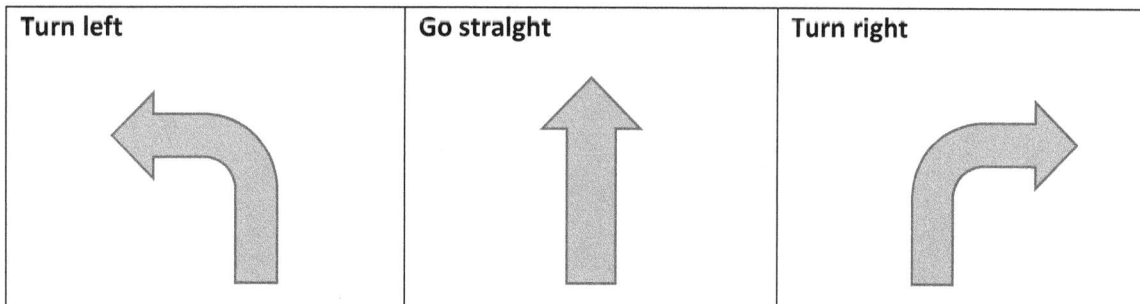

Turn left	Go straight	Turn right
←	↑	→

Other vocabulary and phrases:

Go straight on...
Go straight until you come to...
Go along...
It is at the end of...

Go back...
Cross at...
It is next to...
It is across from...

It is between... and...
Take (this street) to...
It is on the left/right...
It is on the corner of...

Direction Words

Turn left	Go straight	Turn right
←	↑	→

Other vocabulary and phrases:

Go straight on...
Go straight until you come to...
Go along...
It is at the end of...

Go back...
Cross at...
It is next to...
It is across from...

It is between... and...
Take (this street) to...
It is on the left/right...
It is on the corner of...

Other materials: None

Activity: Have students rotate around the room, asking the questions. When the other person answers (preferably in complete sentences), put his name in the appropriate *adverb* column.

How often do you....

	Never	Rarely	Sometimes	Usually	Always
Call your family?					√ (Name)
Clean the house?					
Cook dinner?					
Drive a car?					
Eat cheese?					
Floss?					
Go to the store?					
Make the bed?					
Mow the lawn?					
Play at the park?					
Ride a bike?					
See movies?					
Shave?					
Sing in the shower?					
Take out the trash?					
Travel by plane?					
Vacation at the beach?					
Vacuum?					
Walk the dog?					
Water the plants?					

SPOONS

Other materials: Spoons

Activity: Place spoons in the middle of the table (one less than the total number of players). Deal each player 4 cards, and place all other cards into a pile. The dealer starts by drawing a card from the pile. If he wants to keep it, he discards one of his other cards to the player to his right. If he does not want it, he passes the card to the right. The player to the right picks up the card and chooses whether to keep or discard to the right. Each player should only have four cards in his hand. The dealer continues quickly to draw and discard cards, so many cards are in play. The first person to make a sentence (subject + verb + *infinitive* + object) takes a spoon. Everyone else follows. The person left without a spoon is out of the game. The rounds continue until one person remains.

I	We	They
She	He	It

Spoons

Spoons

Spoons

Spoons

Spoons

Spoons

I	We	You (Singular)
She	He	It
We	They	You (Plural)

Spoons

Spoons

Spoons

Spoons

Spoons

Spoons

Spoons

Spoons

Spoons

Want	Need	Would like
Agree	Decided	Expect
Hope	Intend	Plan

Spoons

Spoons

Spoons

Spoons

Spoons

Spoons

Spoons

Spoons

Spoons

Wants	Needs	Would like
Agrees	Decided	Expects
Hopes	Intends	Plans

Spoons

Spoons

Spoons

Spoons

Spoons

Spoons

Spoons

Spoons

Spoons

Prefer	Promise	Refuse
Remember	Seem	Tend
Try	Wish	Begin

Spoons	Spoons	Spoons
Spoons	Spoons	Spoons
Spoons	Spoons	Spoons

Prefers	Promises	Refuses
Remembers	Seems	Tends
Tries	Wishes	Begins

Spoons

Spoons

Spoons

Spoons

Spoons

Spoons

Spoons

Spoons

Spoons

Remember	Agree	Appear
Remembers	Agrees	Appears
Ask	Like	Expect

Spoons

Spoons

Spoons

Spoons

Spoons

Spoons

Spoons

Spoons

Spoons

Asks	Likes	Expects
(Your idea)	(Your idea)	(Your idea)
(Your idea)	(Your idea)	(Your idea)

Spoons

Spoons

Spoons

Spoons

Spoons

Spoons

Spoons

Spoons

Spoons

To plant	To run	To walk
To eat	To marry	To play
To listen	To encourage	To decorate

Spoons

Spoons

Spoons

Spoons

Spoons

Spoons

Spoons

Spoons

Spoons

To avoid	To go	To call
To draw	To laugh	To understand
To return	To visit	To build

Spoons

Spoons

Spoons

Spoons

Spoons

Spoons

Spoons

Spoons

Spoons

To hear	To shower	To make
To keep	To work	To buy
To try	To see	To cook

Spoons	Spoons	Spoons
Spoons	Spoons	Spoons
Spoons	Spoons	Spoons

To do	To get	To adopt
To accept	To shut	To meet
To sell	To gather	To receive

Spoons

Spoons

Spoons

Spoons

Spoons

Spoons

Spoons

Spoons

Spoons

To love	To talk	To drive
To sleep	To borrow	To use
(Your idea)	(Your idea)	(Your idea)

Spoons	Spoons	Spoons
Spoons	Spoons	Spoons
Spoons	Spoons	Spoons

Homework	Pizza	The door
Home	The highway	Breakfast
A new job	12 hours	A gift

Spoons	Spoons	Spoons
Spoons	Spoons	Spoons
Spoons	Spoons	Spoons

Her	A ball	The morning
A joke	Laundry	A raise
A fight	A masterpiece	The piano

Spoons

Spoons

Spoons

Spoons

Spoons

Spoons

Spoons

Spoons

Spoons

Milk	A donation	To Memphis
A dog	This building	Everything
A dream job	To the radio	To her house

Spoons

Spoons

Spoons

Spoons

Spoons

Spoons

Spoons

Spoons

Spoons

The dishes	Something new	A mansion
Later	Before lunch	There
A play	Football	Anywhere

Spoons

Spoons

Spoons

Spoons

Spoons

Spoons

Spoons

Spoons

Spoons

A memory	To the park	To the mall
Some exercise	A new car	A notebook
Her dad	One day	The sunset

Spoons

Spoons

Spoons

Spoons

Spoons

Spoons

Spoons

Spoons

Spoons

Around the block	A marathon	Tomorrow
To the store	Eggs	Ice cream
Anyone	The sights	The love of his life

Spoons

Spoons

Spoons

Spoons

Spoons

Spoons

Spoons

Spoons

Spoons

Library books	A house	The museum
Donuts	A castle	A full meal
The tuba	Him	French fries

Spoons

Spoons

Spoons

Spoons

Spoons

Spoons

Spoons

Spoons

Spoons

Her parents	Berlin	The zoo
Today	A movie	A meeting
Them	All the time	tennis

Spoons	Spoons	Spoons
Spoons	Spoons	Spoons
Spoons	Spoons	Spoons

A haircut	A garden	A boat
A big truck	An errand	Chickens
Next year	His mom	To his favorite song

Spoons

Spoons

Spoons

Spoons

Spoons

Spoons

Spoons

Spoons

Spoons

(Your idea)

Spoons

Spoons

Spoons

Spoons

Spoons

Spoons

Spoons

Spoons

Spoons

CONSTRUCTING SENTENCES

Other materials: None

Activity: Place all cards on a table. Have students work together to make sentences with the *infinitive*.

I	You	We
He	She	It
They	Want	Wants
Need	Needs	Intend

Plan	Plans	Intends
Hope	Hopes	Would like
Expect	Expects	To work
To go	To shower	To walk

To meet	To see	To sell
To do	To try	To cook
To play	To run	To sleep
To eat	To get	To buy

To visit	To talk	To plan
To take	A raise	A television
A new job	homework	An errand
Basketball	A nap	flowers

To heaven	To the bank	To the mall
To the store	Something new	The guitar
A boat	The museum	A new car
The sunset	To Paris	The zoo

The dishes	Sushi	A watch
A haircut	A house	A marathon
The piano	His mom	laundry
London	Soccer	sugar

MODELING MODALS

Other materials: None

Activity: Divide students into partners or groups. Have one student draw a "problem" card and the other a "solution" one, completing the sentence with his own idea, using a **modal verb**.

I got stung by a bee.	My baby will not stop crying.
Someone ate my lunch.	My son did not make the team.
The neighbors keep throwing loud parties.	I am very tired.

The problem is...

The problem is...

The problem is...

The problem is...

The problem is...

The problem is...

I do not have enough money to pay my rent.	My child is misbehaving at school.	I have a flat tire.
My spouse and I had an argument.	I feel lonely.	I was late for an important meeting.
I burned my dinner.	I lost my wallet and keys.	My friend was diagnosed with cancer.

The
problem
is...

The
problem
is...

The
problem
is...

The
problem
is...

The
problem
is...

The
problem
is...

The
problem
is...

The
problem
is...

The
problem
is...

My air conditioning will not work.	I dropped my phone!	I broke a nail.
I was in a car accident.	This person keeps gossiping about me.	I am not sleeping well.
Someone broke into my home.	I do not know where I am.	My Internet is super slow.

The
problem
is...

The
problem
is...

The
problem
is...

The
problem
is...

The
problem
is...

The
problem
is...

The
problem
is...

The
problem
is...

The
problem
is...

I have come down with flu.	My house is really dirty.	I cannot seem to find a new job.
I do not have enough time to do everything!	My teacher keeps telling me to speak English.	I cannot fit into my pants.
(Your idea)	(Your idea)	(Your idea)

The
problem
is...

The
problem
is...

The
problem
is...

The
problem
is...

The
problem
is...

The
problem
is...

The
problem
is...

The
problem
is...

The
problem
is...

You have to...	You should...	You could...
You have to...	You should...	You could...
You have to...	You should...	You could...

Hmmm...

Hmmm...

Hmmm...

Hmmm...

Hmmm...

Hmmm...

Hmmm...

Hmmm...

Hmmm...

You must...	You ought to...	You might...
You must...	You ought to...	You might...
You must...	You ought to...	You might...

Hmmm...

Hmmm...

Hmmm...

Hmmm...

Hmmm...

Hmmm...

Hmmm...

Hmmm...

Hmmm...

YOU'RE SWEET

Other materials: Any kind of colored candy pieces

Activity: Divide students into partners or groups. Have each take some candy and complete sentences about themselves for each candy taken.

Candy Colors

Red: I hate it when...

Orange: I love to eat...

Yellow: I am happy when...

Green: I wish I had a...

Blue: Something that makes me sad is...

Brown: One of my hobbies is...

Purple: A good friend is...

Candy Colors

Red: I hate it when...

Orange: I love to eat...

Yellow: I am happy when...

Green: I wish I had a...

Blue: Something that makes me sad is...

Brown: One of my hobbies is...

Purple: A good friend is...

Candy Colors

Red: I hate it when...

Orange: I love to eat...

Yellow: I am happy when...

Green: I wish I had a...

Blue: Something that makes me sad is...

Brown: One of my hobbies is...

Purple: A good friend is...

Candy Colors

Red: I hate it when...

Orange: I love to eat...

Yellow: I am happy when...

Green: I wish I had a...

Blue: Something that makes me sad is...

Brown: One of my hobbies is...

Purple: A good friend is...

GETTING TO KNOW YOU

Other materials: Possible key rings, bags

Activity: Place all questions in a bag (or put them on a key ring). Have students partner-up and ask whatever question they draw to **get to know** their partners.

What is your name?	Do you have any children?
Where are you from?	Where do you live?
What kind of music do you like?	What do you like to do for fun?
What do you and your friends do together?	What do you do for work?
When is your birthday?	Do you have a pet? What kind?

How are you doing today?	Tell me about your country.
Do you play any instruments? Which ones?	What sports do you play?
What time do you normally wake up?	How many siblings do you have?
What countries have you visited?	Ask any question. (Your idea)

Got a Favorite?

Other materials: Possible key rings, bags

Activity: Place all questions in a bag (or put them on a key ring). Have students partner-up and ask each other their *favorites* and why.

What is your Favorite outfit?
Bonus: Why?

What is your Favorite book?
Bonus: Why?

What is your Favorite instrument?
Bonus: Why?

What is your Favorite chore?
Bonus: Why?

Favorites

Favorites

Favorites

Favorites

What is your Favorite Food?
Bonus: Why?

What is your Favorite Sport?
Bonus: Why?

What is your Favorite TV Show?
Bonus: Why?

What is your Favorite game?
Bonus: Why?

What is your Favorite color?
Bonus: Why?

What is your Favorite animal?
Bonus: Why?

What is your Favorite Season?
Bonus: Why?

What is your Favorite Movie?
Bonus: Why?

Favorites

Favorites

Favorites

Favorites

Favorites

Favorites

Favorites

Favorites

What is your Favorite Fruit?
Bonus: Why?

Who is your Favorite actor/actress?
Bonus: Why?

What is your Favorite Hobby?
Bonus: Why?

Who is your Favorite person?
Bonus: Why?

What is your Favorite place?
Bonus: Why?

Who is your Favorite Singer?
Bonus: Why?

What is your Favorite dessert?
Bonus: Why?

What is your Favorite Store?
Bonus: Why?

Favorites

Favorites

Favorites

Favorites

Favorites

Favorites

Favorites

Favorites

WHY, OH WHY?

Other materials: None

Activity: Have students ask and answer *why* questions using because or because of.

Why....?	Because..../ Because of...
Why are you here?	
Why do you call 911?	
Why do you cry?	
Why do you eat?	
Why do you exercise?	
Why do you get haircuts?	
Why do you get scared?	
Why do you go to school?	
Why do you go to the dentist?	
Why do you go to the hospital?	
Why do you go to work?	
Why do you laugh?	
Why do you see movies?	
Why do you shower?	
Why do you sleep?	
Why do you stress?	
Why do you sweat?	
Why do you watch television?	

TWENTY QUESTIONS

Other materials: Paper strips, markers

Activity: Have one person come to the front of the room and write a noun on a piece of paper. Have other students ask **Yes/No questions** to figure out the noun. If no one guesses after twenty tries, the answer will be revealed.

Extra: This can also be a competition where a questioner gets to ask another question each time he receives a "yes" response. "No" passes to the next player.

Here are some examples of Yes/No questions:

- Are you human?

- Are you famous?

- Are you in this school? library?

- Are you in this building? classroom?

- Are you a man? woman?

- Are you a food?

- Can I eat you?

- Can you fly?

- Do you talk?

- Are you sugary? salty? tasty?

- Are you big? small?

- Are you bigger/smaller than a _____ (object/animal)?

- Are you an animal?

- Do you live in _____ (place)?

- Are you _____ (color)?

- Are you an object?

- Are you made of _____ (material)?

LET US LABEL TOGETHER

Other materials: Tape

Activity: Work with students to label the *classroom* together.

Table	Chair	Desk
Book	Pencil	Computer
Poster	Outlet	Door
Window	Calendar	Eraser
Marker	Whiteboard	Chalkboard
Chalk	Clock	Cabinet

Vying for Vocabuarly

Other materials: Whiteboard, markers, bag, timer

Activity: Draw a category from a bag. Have students work in teams to write down as many words as possible within a certain time limit. Cross out words both teams have written. The team with the most **vocabulary** words remaining gets the point.

Adjectives
Animals
Articles of Clothing
Breakfast Foods
Daily Activities
Fruits
Items Around the House
Places Around Town
Toys
Types of Movies
Types of Restaurants
Vegetables
Verbs

NAME THAT PROFESSION

Other materials: Clothes pins

Activity: Pin a profession to the back of each student's shirt. Without saying the word, have other students *describe the profession* until the student guesses what it is.

MUSICIAN

FARMER

DENTIST

WAITER

MECHANIC

ATHLETE

POLICE OFFICER

SINGER

PILOT

ACTOR

SCIENTIST

DOCTOR

VET

TEACHER

FIREFIGHTER

MINER

Taboo

Other materials: Bag

Activity: Have a student draw a *word* from a bag and describe the word until the other students guess what it is.

Chair	Banana
Book	Door
Fish	Pillow
Ball	Map
Fork	Sweater

Star	Penguin
Computer	Sunglasses
Elephant	Joke

Taboo redux

Other materials: Bag

Activity: Have a student draw a *word* from a bag and describe the word until the other students guess what it is.

BICYCLE	CANDLE
SOFA	SUGAR
SOAP	INTERNET
HORSE	CHOCOLATE
DUCK	HOSPITAL

SOUP	NECKLACE
RAZOR	SODA
CALENDAR	PLAYGROUND
TEDDY BEAR	SANDWICH
LAMP	LEMON

CARD TABOO

Other materials: Bag

Activity: Divide students into teams. Have one person from a team draw a list from the bag. Set the timer. The person must describe the **word** without saying it or using gestures. If the word is unknown, the student can pass to the next word. The team gets a point for every word guessed correctly.

In the Kitchen	All Business	Teach Me, Please
- Fork	- Post Office	- Books
- Refrigerator	- Grocery store	- Homework
- Pot	- Bank	- Chalkboard
- Blender	- Nail salon	- Desks
- Stove	- Restaurant	- Posters
- Glass/Cup	- Movie theater	- Erasers
- Plate	- Electronic store	- Computer
- Knife	- Mall	- Markers
- Napkin	- Fast food joint	- Games
- Spoon	- Shoe shop	- Tests
Wild Kingdom	**What to Wear**	**What shall I learn?**
- Bear	- Socks	- Math
- Zebra	- Pajamas	- History
- Lion	- Skirt	- Drama
- Deer	- Tie	- Science
- Raccoon	- Bathrobe	- P.E. (or gym)
- Giraffe	- Pants	- Literature
- Tiger	- Hat	- Art
- Rhinoceros	- Shoes	- Government
- Elephant	- Belt	- Music
- Fox	- Bathing suit	- Cooking
In House	**Bone-to-Bone**	**Getting Fruity**
- Closet	- Elbow	- Apple
- Kitchen	- Head	- Grapes
- Garage	- Wrist	- Banana
- Livingroom	- Leg	- Pineapple
- Study	- Nose	- Orange
- Bathroom	- Toes	- Mango
- Bedroom	- Neck	- Lemon
- Foyer	- Arm	- Peach
- Laundry room	- Mouth	- Blueberry
- Backyard	- Shoulders	- Pear

PYRAMID

Other materials: Bag or computer presentation program, timer

Activity: Divide students into teams. Have one person from a team draw a list from the bag. Set the timer. The person must describe the **word** without saying it or using gestures. If the word is unknown, the student can pass to the next word. The team gets a point for every word guessed correctly.

Extra: Input words onto individual slides in a presentation software and play like the Pyramid game. Click through slides as words are guessed or passed over.

A Little Healthy Competition (Sports and Activities We Play)	**Don't Toy With Me (Different Kinds of Toys)**
- Tennis	- Boat
- Basketball	- Rubberduck
- Soccer	- Armyman
- Car racing	- Babydoll
- Board games	- Barbie
- Horseshoes	- Stuffed animal
- Skiing	- Building blocks
- Gymnastics	- Puzzle
- Swimming	- Toaster oven
- Football	- Trampoline
Animal House (Pets People Keep)	**Relax, Pal (What People Do or Use to Relieve Stress)**
- Dog	- Pillow
- Cat	- Bed
- Parakeet	- Recliner
- Goldfish	- Get a massage
- Mouse	- Take a hot bath
- Hamster	- Do aerobics
- Horse	- Take a nap
- Turtle	- Hang out with friends
- Snake	- Eat
- Tarantula	- Watch a movie
Aren't You Sweet (Tasty Sugary Morsels)	**Let's Make Up (Different Types of Make-up)**
- Cookies	- Lipstick
- Birthday cake	- Foundation
- Sundae	- Eyeliner
- Chocolate	- Mascara
- Banana split	- Blush
- Popsicle	- Nail polish
- Cheesecake	- Eye shadow
- Pie	- Highlighter
- Ice cream	- Lipliner
- Marshmallow	- Concealer

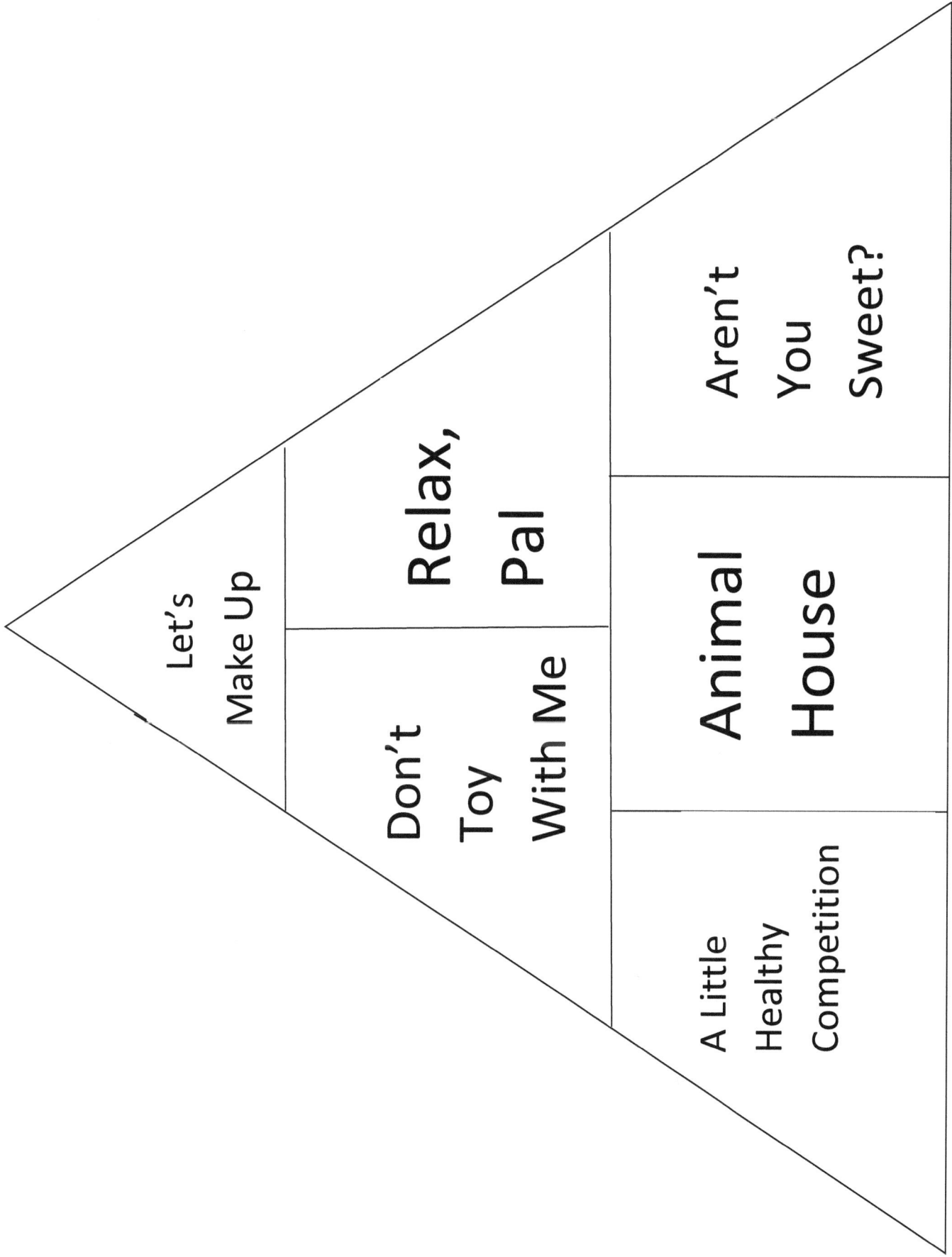

Let's
Make Up

Relax,
Pal

Don't
Toy
With Me

Aren't
You
Sweet?

Animal
House

A Little
Healthy
Competition

Pyramid

Pyramid — take two

Other materials: Bag or computer presentation program, timer

Activity: Divide students into teams. Have one person from a team draw a list from the bag. Set the timer. The person must describe the *word* without saying it or using gestures. If the word is unknown, the student can pass to the next word. The team gets a point for every word guessed correctly.

Extra: Input words onto individual slides in a presentation software and play like the Pyramid game. Click through slides as words are guessed or passed over

A Bit of Class (Typical Items Found in a Classroom)	Call the Geek Squad (Types and Terms of Technology)
- Whiteboard	- Cell phone
- Eraser	- Computer
- Desks or tables	- I-pad
- Chair	- MP3 player
- Books	- Radio
- Markers	- DVD
- Lesson	- Laptop
- Homework	- Printer
- Tests	- Virus
- Syllabus	- Troubleshoot
Let's Do Lunch **(What You Might Grab Around Noon)**	**The Style Guide** **(What We Wear)**
- Sandwich	- T-shirt
- Salad	- Blouse
- Pizza	- Sneakers
- Pasta	- Coat
- Taco	- Hat
- Hamburger	- High heels
- Chicken nuggets	- Jeans
- Fruit	- Poncho
- Soda	- Scarf
- Lunchbox	- Accessories
Out of this World **(Stuff You Find in the Sky)**	**Feel the Rhythm** **(Types of Music)**
- Birds	- Country western
- Sun	- Rap
- Moon	- Classical
- Stars	- Pop
- Planets	- Rock
- Planes	- Jazz
- Spaceships	- Alternative
- Meteors	- Heavy metal
- The Galaxy	- Indie
- Drones	- Acapella

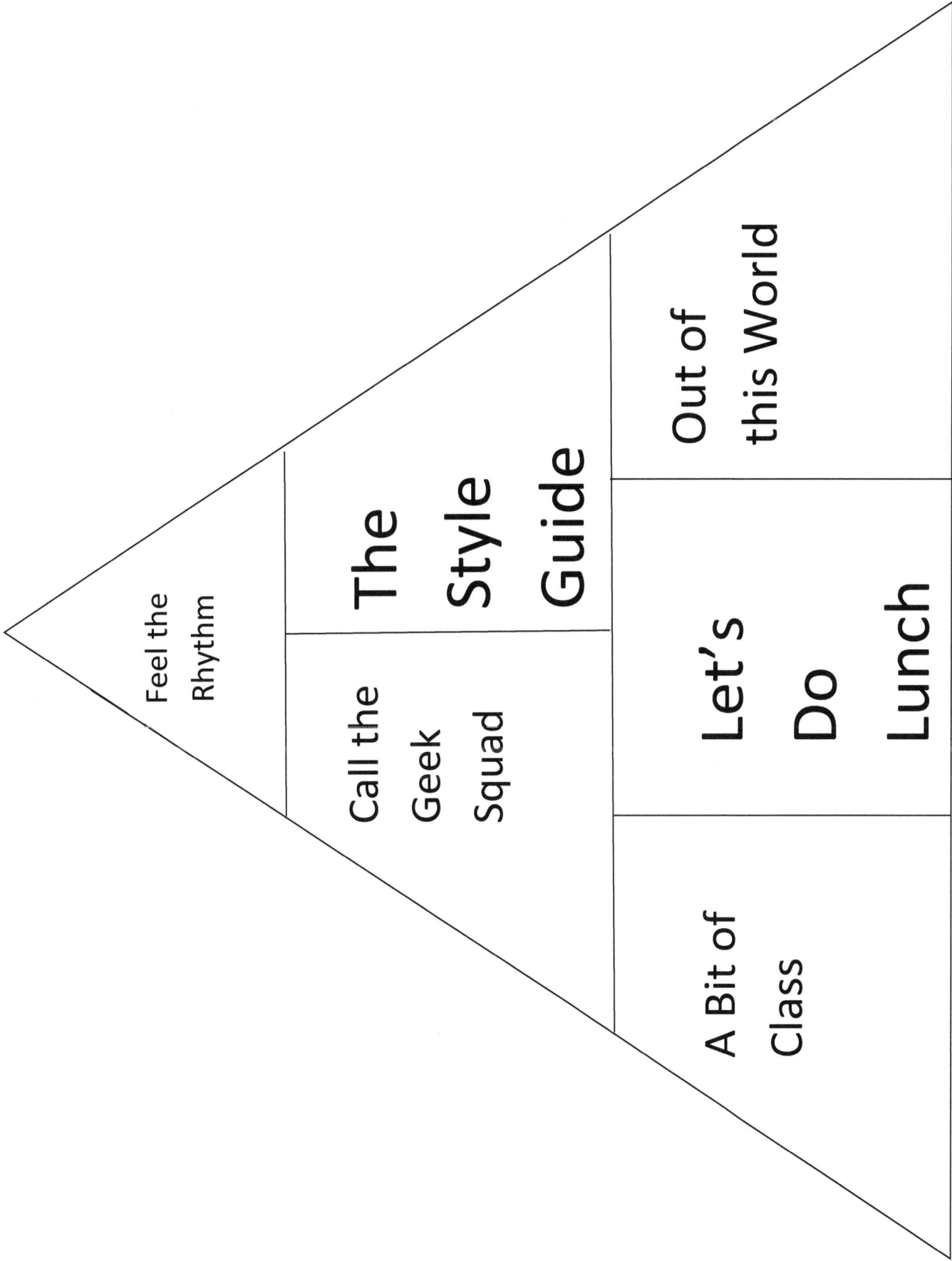

Feel the
Rhythm

Call the
Geek
Squad

The
Style
Guide

A Bit of
Class

Let's
Do
Lunch

Out of
this World

Pyramid

NAME THAT MEDIA

Other materials: Bag

Activity: Have a student draw a media type. The student thinks of a specific example, and without saying the title, describes the movie/TV show/song/book to the class until they **guess the name** of it.

Movie	Movie	Movie
TV Show	TV Show	TV Show
Song	Song	Song
Book	Book	Book

AGREE TO DISAGREE

Other materials: Tape

Activity: Tape the Agree, Somewhat Agree, Disagree, and Somewhat Agree signs in separate corners of the room. Read one of the statements below. Have students go to the corner that represents how they feel and take turns *explaining* why they feel that way.

Pizza would be great for breakfast.
Movie stars should get paid more money.
Sports stars should get paid less money.
You should vote in every election.
People should be allowed to vote by phone.
You should get a flu shot every winter.
Sports games should be held on Saturdays.
Never use public transportation.
There should be no speed limits on roads.
College education should be free.
The Citizenship process should be simplified.
Everyone should learn how to speak English.
It's okay if we end class an hour early.
Today is a wonderful day for a picnic.
Soccer is the world's best sport.

You should always go to bed early.
It's alright if you're never on time.
Life would be perfect if everyone had a million dollars.

SOMEWHAT SOMEWHAT
AGREE

AGREE

SOMEWHAT
DISAGREE

DISAGREE

FAMILY TREE

Other materials: Family tree (on a large poster board), Velcro

Activity: Have students **work together** to figure out where family members go on the family tree based on the clues provided.

Charlie met Edith when he returned from World War II.
They have three children, twin granddaughters, and one grand-dog that they adore!
Mike was the best man at his little brother's wedding.
Kiana is Sharon's sister-in-law.

Between law school and work, Robert and his new wife have been super busy.

Karen hasn't known Shelley and Kelly very long.

Sharon absolutely loves being an aunt to her brother's kids.

The youngest child shares an apartment with a four~legged friend.

George likes to go walking every morning and evening.

He likes to eat beef, chicken, and other people food.

They were born on the same day.

Shelley is best friends with her sister.

CHARLIE

EDITH

MIKE

KIANA

ROBERT

KAREN

SHARON

GEORGE

SHELLEY

KELLY

The Family Tree

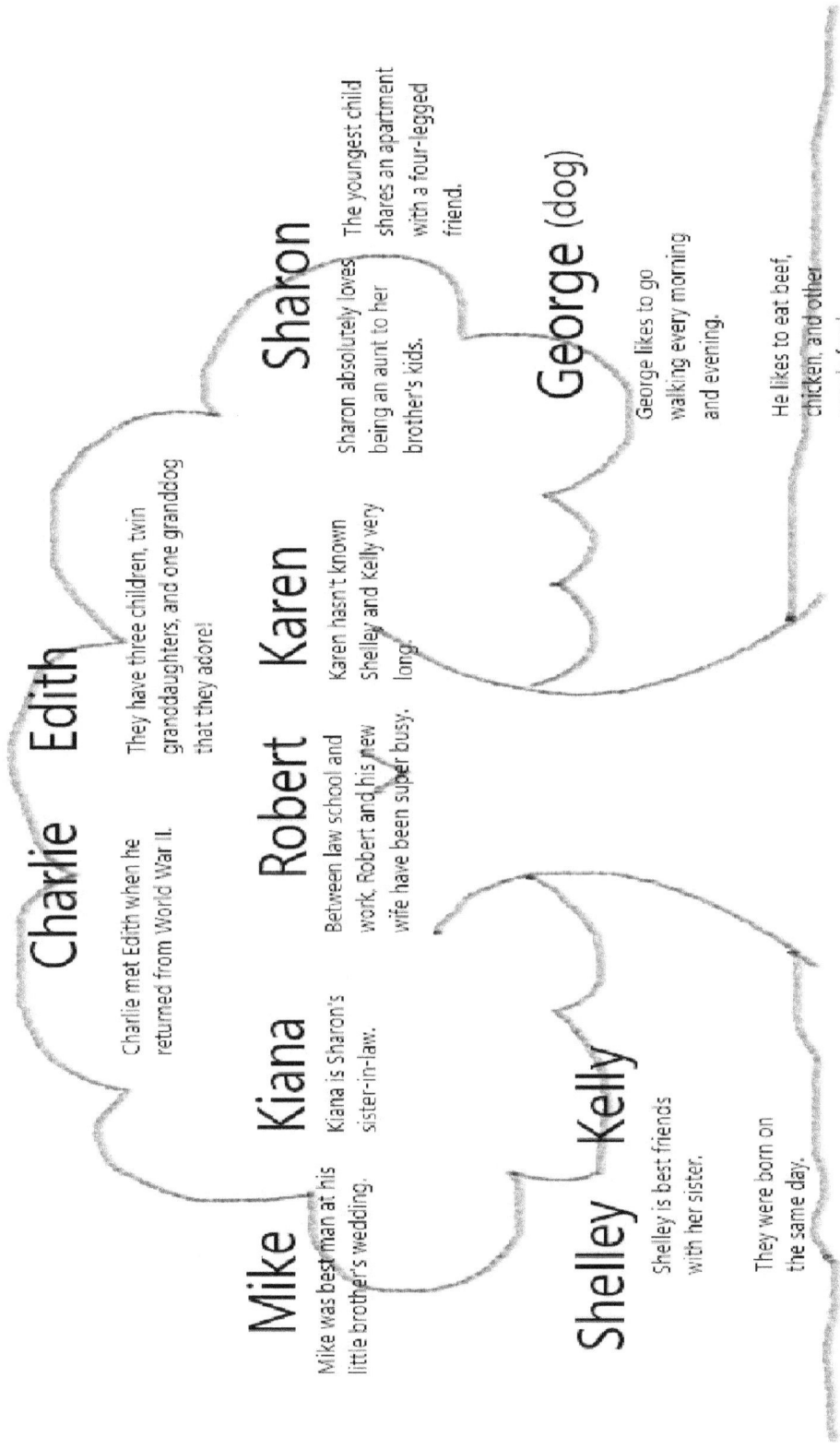

Mike

Mike was best man at his little brother's wedding.

Kiana

Kiana is Sharon's sister-in-law.

Charlie   Edith

Charlie met Edith when he returned from World War II.

They have three children, twin granddaughters, and one granddog that they adore!

Robert

Between law school and work, Robert and his new wife have been super busy.

Karen

Karen hasn't known Shelley and Kelly very long.

Sharon

Sharon absolutely loves being an aunt to her brother's kids.

The youngest child shares an apartment with a four-legged friend.

Shelley   Kelly

Shelley is best friends with her sister.

They were born on the same day.

George (dog)

George likes to go walking every morning and evening.

He likes to eat beef, chicken, and other people food.

Other materials: None

Activity: Break students into partners and have them practice *interviewing* one another. One will act as interviewer (using the questions below); the other as interviewee. Then have them switch roles.

JOB INTERVIEW QUESTIONS
Tell me about yourself...
Why should we hire you?
What is your greatest strength?
What is your greatest weakness?
Why do you want to work for us?
Why did you leave your last job?
What is your greatest accomplishment?
Describe a difficult situation and what you did to overcome it...
Where do you see yourself in 5 years?
Do you have any questions for me?

A SPACE ADVENTURE

Other materials: Bag

Activity: Have each student draw a job. Based on what is drawn, the student will "**present a case**" before the captains to go into space. At the end of all the arguments, the captain(s) will confer and decide which people are going on the adventure.

Janitor	Defense Specialist
Program Organizer	Mechanic
Entertainer	Lawyer
Cook	Computer Expert
Manager	Doctor

A Space Adventure

_____ captains are about to go on an amazing, but somewhat risky, adventure to space, and YOU would really like to go! The problem is they can only take _____ other people. So now you you must present your case before the captains to ensure they pick you! Good luck!

And may the force be with you!

Musical Chairs

Other materials: Chairs, music

Activity: Arrange chairs into a circle, one minus the total number of students. Give students a category. Call out words specific to that category while students rotate around the chairs. Students will take a chair as soon as they hear unrelated words. The person left without a chair is out of the *game*. This process continues until one student remains.

Sample categories:

Fruits	Vegetables	Furniture	Past Tense Verbs	Adjectives
Apples	Carrots	Chair	Walked	Beautiful
Bananas	Green beans	Sofa	Talked	Pretty
Pineapple	Peas	Ottoman	Jumped	Green
Mango	Beets	Table	Built	Yellow
Grapes	Corn	Desk	Fled	Short
Starfruit	Lettuce	Lamp	Ran	Tall
Papaya	Broccoli	Loveseat	Called	Fat
Coconut	Squash	End table	Spoke	Small
Pears	Asparagus	Stool	Said	Skinny
Peaches	Zucchini	Shelf	Did	Fast
Cantaloupe	Spinach	TV stand	Ate	Nice
Honeydew	Green pepper	Entertainment	Went	Sweet
Watermelon	Yellow pepper	center	Left	Sour
Grapefruit	Red pepper	Bed	Showered	Tasty
Strawberries	Mushroom	Dresser	Dressed	Smart
Blueberries	Cucumber	Nightstand	Played	Smelly
Blackberries	Lima beans	TV tray	Baked	Aromatic
Raspberries	Okra		Cooked	Pleasant
Apricots	Cabbage		Let	Clever
Plums	Radish		Came	Fun
Pomegranate	Cauliflower		Swept	Colorful
Cherries			Whispered	Clean
Lemon			Hugged	Dirty
Lime			Tried	Big
			Studied	Bad
			Burned	Good
			Kept	Horrible
			Showed	Crazy
			Swam	
			Wrote	
			Drew	
			Drank	
			Brushed	
			Exercised	
			Threw	
			Read	

PROVERB PICTIONARY

Other materials: Whiteboard, marker, eraser, bag, timer

Activity: Provide a copy of the proverbs to each student. Have a student draw a proverb out of a bag and come to the board. Set the timer for however long desired. Have the student *draw* the proverb to the best of his ability while the other students guess.

Don't look a gift horse in the mouth. (Don't find fault with a received gift or favor.)	**A friend in need is a friend indeed!** (A person who helps in difficult times is a truly reliable person.)	**Don't put off until tomorrow what you can do today.** (Don't procrastinate!)
The early bird catches the worm. (The first person to arrive has the best chance for success.)	**Where there is a will there is always a way.** (If you are determined, you can achieve what you want, even if it is very difficult!)	**The patient dog gets the bone.** (Patience is rewarding.)
Every cloud has a silver lining. (Difficult times lead to better days.)	**It is better to have loved and lost than never to have loved at all.** (Exactly what it says.)	**A disappointment is a blessing.** (We can turn bad moments into positive opportunities.)
A bird in hand is worth two in the bush. (Be happy with what you, instead of risking everything for something more.)	**More haste less speed.** (There is more progress when you don't try to do something too quickly.)	**Don't judge a book by its cover.** (Don't prejudge something by outward appearance alone.)

The Family Game

- START
- Is your family big or small?
- How many brothers and sisters do you have?
- Free
- Talk about your mother.
- Go forward three spaces.
- Are you the oldest, middle, or youngest child?
- Are you married?
- How long have you been married?
- Go back two spaces.
- How many children do you have?
- Share a story about your grandparents.
- Go forward two spaces.
- Do you have family reunions?
- Describe your father.
- What is your favorite family tradition?
- Does your family live nearby?
- Free
- Free
- Who do you call when you need help?
- Talk about your childhood.
- Go forward two spaces.
- Share a story about your children.
- What makes your family laugh?
- What is one thing you always do as a family?
- Go back three spaces.
- Where has your family gone for vacation?
- Do you have a pet?
- Free
- Go back three spaces.
- FINISH

LET'S TALK "THE FUTURE"

FINISH	MY GOALS: I _____ ...	
Your thoughts...		
SHE _____ WITH HER PARENTS.	NEXT TIME, THEY _____	
MOVE FORWARD TWO SPACES.		
NO, YOU _____ THAT!		
MOVE BACKWARD FOUR SPACES.	FOR DINNER TONIGHT, SHE _____ .	

MOVE BACKWARD THREE SPACES.	THIS YEAR, WE _____ ...	NEVER! IT _____ ...
WE _____ DURING THE HOLIDAYS.	I _____ SOMETIME THIS YEAR.	

HE _____ THIS WEEK.

Will or Won't?

YOU _____ ON SATURDAY.

THEY _____ IN THE MORNING.

MOVE FORWARD TWO SPACES.	YOU WILL _____ NEXT YEAR.	IT WON'T _____ TOMORROW.
I WILL GET HOME AT _____ TODAY.	WE WILL _____ IN THE FUTURE.	
START	SHE WON'T _____ LATER.	MOVE BACKWARD THREE SPACES.
THEY WILL _____ SOON.	IT WON'T _____ FOR CHRISTMAS.	MOVE FORWARD THREE SPACES.

Add a base verb!

Remember: Subject + Will + Base Verb...

Tell Me The Future

START	HOW OLD WILL YOU BE NEXT YEAR?	MOVE FORWARD TWO SPACES.
ARE YOU GOING TO WATCH TV LATER?	WHAT WILL THE WEATHER BE LIKE TOMORROW?	WHEN WILL YOU GET HOME?
MOVE BACKWARD THREE SPACES.		FREE
WHO WILL YOU CONTACT SOON?	WHERE WILL YOU GO ON SATURDAY?	
WHAT WILL YOU DO THIS WEEK?	MOVE FORWARD THREE SPACES.	ARE YOU DOING ANYTHING IN THE MORNING?

FREE	HOW WILL YOU CELEBRATE THE HOLIDAYS?	ARE YOU PLANNING ANYTHING SPECIAL THIS YEAR?

MOVE BACKWARD THREE SPACES.	WILL YOU COME TO CLASS NEXT TIME?	FINISH
WHERE ARE YOU TRAVELING TO THIS YEAR?	FREE	WHEN ARE YOU GOING TO CALL YOUR PARENTS?
WILL IT SNOW FOR CHRISTMAS?		MOVE FORWARD TWO SPACES.
	WHAT WILL YOU EAT FOR DINNER TONIGHT?	WHEN WILL YOU RUN YOUR ERRANDS?
		MOVE BACKWARD FOUR SPACES.

WHY? WHY? WHY?

Start 1	I'm tired because...	She is happy because of...	S1 → / S2 →	I like school because of...	We can't play tennis because...	Start 2
I don't want to go outside because of...			I don't like politics because...			They like pizza because of...
We are hungry because...	They love their teacher because...	We exercise every day because of...	← S1 / S2 →	You are angry because of...	Because / Because of...	English is important because...
She enjoys shopping because of...			← S2 / S1 →	Remember: Because + noun + verb / Because of + noun phrase	↓ S2 / S1 →	He needs money because...
		They cancelled coming because...		He doesn't like driving because of...	I take English classes because...	We don't watch T.V. because of...
Finish	My family is important because....	I hate _____ because...		Want to change things up? Move the clause to the front! *Because I am happy, I smile. Because of this game, I feel better.*		I love _____ because of...
						Finish

BACK IN BLACK

Other materials: Timer, (possible) alphabet die

Activity: Pick a letter or roll an alphabet die. Have teams work together to write down as many words as they can for each category that start with that letter. Whoever lists the most or gets one for each column *wins* the round.

Noun	Verb	Past Participle	Adjective	Adverb

Start

Finish

START				

FINISH

Finish

Start

Idea #1 Skit/Play

- Write a short play/skit, to include characters and dialogue. Your play can be funny, scary, romantic, serious, historical, etc. Try to incorporate at least 5 vocabulary words and some of the grammatical structures we have studied.

  Talk it out with your group! And remember to HAVE FUN!

Idea #2 Illustrated Short Story

- With your group, create an illustrated short story (like a children's story). Discuss with your team what you want your story to be about and how you would like it to be drawn. Try to incorporate vocabulary and grammar from chapters we have studied. Aim for about 10 pages. Illustrations do *not* have to be complicated. Make sure everyone in the group participates.

  Each group will present his story at the end of class.

Idea #3 New Product/Feature

- With your group, create a new product or add new features to an existing one. Make a print advertisement showcasing your creation. Create a commercial to talk about and sell your product. Be ready to present it to the class.

Idea #4 Plan a Party

With your group, plan a party for 20 people. Consider the following questions:

- What kind of party do you want to have?

- When and where will it be?

- Will there be music? What genre? Live or DJ?

- Will there be any kind of entertainment or games? Are kids invited?

- Will there be food? If so, what kind and how much? Homemade or catered?

- Will there be decorations? What type?

- What supplies do you need?

- Are you planning to have party favors or gifts? If so, describe.

- How much money are you planning to spend?

Make a detailed budget/supply list and create an invitation.

Idea #5

Create your ideal city. What is its name?

What laws, government, food, entertainment, jobs, housing, transportation, language (and so forth) would it have? What would it look like? Make a brochure that describes your city. Include a map or picture.

Be prepared to present your "Utopia" at the end of class.

Idea #6

Your assignment is to create an English language learning game.

Discuss with your group what kind of game you would like to do (IE board game, card game, etc), along with the theme, characters, vocabulary, and grammar.

Write down the game rules.

We will test the games at the end of class.

Doraina Pyle is an author who desires to "Make a positive difference." Much of her time is spent as a volunteer at church and in the community. In 2003, she earned a Dual Bachelor's degree in French Studies and English Composition from the University of North Texas. In 2009, she completed a Master of Arts in Language Acquisition and Teaching at Brigham Young University. For the past six years, she has taught English as a Second Language (ESL) to adult learners online and in the Dallas area. In her spare time, Doraina enjoys reading, dancing, piano, and travel. She is an avid seeker of self-improvement and finds joy in the beauty of living simply. Her previous works include *Walk Through Sprinklers*, *The Curse of Being Pretty (and Other Pitfalls)*, *The Parable of the Weedy Yard*, and *My Mid-Single Mindset*.

For more information, please visit:

https://www.dorainapyle.com/

http://makeapositivedifference.blogspot.com/

www.ingramcontent.com/pod-product-compliance
Lightning Source LLC
LaVergne TN
LVHW081314060426
835509LV00015B/1513